Copyright © 2019 by Raymond Nwachukwu.

Dedication
This Book is dedicated to Entrepreneurs who has been struggling to make money on the Internet.

TABLE OF CONTENT

CPA AFFILIATE MARKETING
(A Beginner's Guide)

INTRODUCTION

In this Short Report, Am going to be Focusing on what you require to implement in a short while to start seeing Results with CPA Affiliate Marketing, even as a Newbie. The Best approach to achieve what is given to you in this book is to take **MASSIVE ACTION.** This report is going to be brief as possible, straight to the point, and a step by step procedures to follow. All you require is to take the necessary **Actions** at each step by the way.

So, if you are ready with me, let's Dive into it...

WHAT IS CPA?

CPA is a form of Affiliate Marketing called Cost per Action. In this form of marketing, the Marketer is paid based on generating leads for the Affiliate Company. These Leads could be in form of Email address, Phone Number, Call or Trial Version of the product and Submission of Credit Card. It is a form of Performance based marketing. You don't have to deal with

Fulfilment, Shipping, Refunds and stuffs like that, so basically, it has Low resistance of entry.

There are Various CPA Affiliate Networks you can Sign Up with, however, some of them require some kind of experience before you can be admitted into them, while some does not require so much experience. Examples of CPA Affiliate Networks you may Sign Up with are: Maxbounty, Peerfly, Adworkmedia, etc. you can just make a little more research on CPA Affiliate Networks and Sign Up with any of them.

Usually, in every Affiliate Network, you are assigned an Affiliate Manager. He/She supposed to be your Best Friend as far as that network is concerned. Most of the time a lot of Affiliates do not utilize their Affiliate Manager Optimally. He would give you insights on some of the Best performing Campaigns inside of the network being promoted by top affiliates and recommend some of the strategies they are using to promote the Offers. After all, as you make more commissions, He/She is also paid higher commissions, so it is a Win-Win for you both.

So here is the deal, once you have discovered the Niche you want to promote, you want to ask your Affiliate Manager these important two Questions:

What is the Best Converting offer in that Niche by these two Metrics?

1) **By Volume:** Of course you do not want to *reinvent the Wheels.* You want to promote what is proven to be already converting.

2) **By EPC:** EPC simply means; earning per click. For example, if you send 100 clicks to an offer and you earn $200, your epc is $2.

You do not need to just focus on the Payout of an offer, because some offers may be converting higher and faster than others, despite their payouts whether high or low.

As a Newbie or beginner, sometimes you may encounter some technical stuffs that probably you don't know how to go about it, now get this; *don't let technicality deter you from achieving your desired results, learn to outsource things and focus on the areas you are good at.* You can outsource on Fiverr or UpWork and get the technical aspect done for you.

Probably, one of your first rock you may be hitting in this journey will be driving Traffic to your offers, but you have to bear this in mind *"on every traffic source, if there are people buying traffic, then, there are people making money".*

There is no magic traffic source, but the secret is to find one, focus tightly until you master it before diversifying to other traffic sources.

TYPES OF OFFERS TO PROMOTE IN CPA AFFILIATE MARKETING

Usually, there are lots of different products one can promote from different Affiliate Networks, but in this Report, we shall recommend just a few.

Maxbounty is a great Affiliate Network to get products to promote. *Use the link below to sign up for an Account if you do not have an Account Yet.*

https://raygoz.com/maxbounty

Peerfly is another great platform to Promote Products from. You can also use the link below to create an Account with them. *https://peerfly.com*

Other platforms includes; www.clickbank.com www.warriorplus.com www.jvzoo.com etc.

There are lots of offers one can promote, but finding the Best offers can be a difficult task. Here are some tips below on how to choose the Best type of Offers you can promote.

1) **Nutraceutical offers (Diet, Testosterone, skin, male enhancement etc):** These are health related type of offers that help people look good, feel good, look younger or solve a particular problem. They are usually *evergreen offers* and usually stand the test of time. These types of offers are proven to work well, especially trial offers, and they have big payouts too. The reason for their high conversion rate is because they address problems related to *self-esteem* and *self-image* of people. Also, people in this type on niche have some sort of **pain or problem** and they are eager for a quick solution. In this case, am not talking about peels, or medications which may take some time before the user starts seeing results, and sometimes these products eventually do not work and are over hyped. Here, I mean products that provides immediate solutions to a particular problem. These people are in pains and need some form of step by step actions to take that will lead them to seeing almost immediate results. It could be a routine

exercise to follow, a Recipe to follow or Diet Plan and stuffs like that. Ordinarily, they could go to a Doctor for solution, but they are searching on the Internet for some sort of immediate solution to follow, or a Practical way that has worked for someone that they can easily follow. These are the type of products you want to be focusing in these type of Niche.

However, bear in mind that these types of offers does require huge budget to test out. It is not very advisable to get into this Niche if you are a Newbie with low budget.

2) **Dating (Mainstream):** Dating Niche is kind of more Newbie friendly. Typically, they are lead generation type of offers. These type of offers have also be proven to convert very well. So, as a Newbie, you might want to start running campaigns in this Niche.

3) **Make Money Online Niche:** This is another great Niche that is very profitable, but you really need to know what you are doing to succeed in this Niche. The Key is to ensure you Give Some Sort of **VALUE** to

your Audience, just like the one I am giving you now...Right? Great!

You can focus on lead generation type of offers especially if you are a Newbie.

4) **Video Sales Letter (VSL):** These are videos that pre-sells offers instead of taking people straight to checkout page. The can actually be within any Niche, but usually, these type of offers does convert well too, so you might also consider running them.

TRAFFIC SOURCES/NETWORKS FOR CPA CAMPAIGNS

This is the most important part of your Marketing. You may have a great Product from the Best Networks, but if no one is seeing them and clicking through, you aren't going to generate any lead or make any sale as the case may be, so pay close attention to this part.

There are different ways to generate traffic on the Internet, but most times affiliates get it all wrong by trying to overcomplicate things and trying to use several Traffic Methods without having a Mastery of

Any. You may have experienced this, jumping from one traffic source to another, especially as it seems the most trending. I also fell for same trap, but have discovered the Best approach which am going to be revealing to you in this Report.

The simple **SECRET is this; FOCUS AND MASTER ONE TRAFFIC SOURCE BEFORE DIVING INTO ANOTHER.** It is that simple, but not easy to be followed, because you will always be tempted to jump around due to the *"Shiny Object Syndrome".* However, if you can be Disciplined enough to follow this simple **SECRET,** you would start seeing tremendous improvement in your Marketing.

You must have heard about several traffic Methods such as Search Traffic, Social Networks, Solo Ads, Email Marketing, Native Ads, Display Networks, etc. Each of them are great, if you really understand the intricacies, but *NEVER* try to jump around again, or you will continue to Burn Your Money and Become Overwhelmed too.

Like I mentioned earlier, there are lots of different traffic sources that one can utilize to generate Revenue with CPA Affiliate Marketing. But the Key is to figure out one, Focus on it and achieve some sort of Mastery before moving to another traffic source. Having said that, let's look at some of the different High Volume traffic sources you can use to generate traffic to your offers.

1) **Native Ads (Content.ad & Revcontent):** These are typical type of ads that you usually see on blogs that are similar to related content, usually with an image and headlines. It is similar to banner advertising, but in this case, blends into the content of the blog. The landing page is usually more of contents and advertorials. However, Native ads do require huge budget to run, but you can actually crush it with these types of traffic sources.

2) **Media Buys (Banner Traffic):** These refers to buying banner traffic. With this type of traffic source, you place banners on websites that has huge traffic, e.g. forbes.com you can go to traffic networks or directly to the website owners to purchase this type of traffic. But as a Newbie, it is more advisable to go to traffic networks so you don't spend so much, test out things and if it works really well, then you can think of going directly to website owners.

Example of Media Buys Traffic Networks include: trafficjunky, adsupply, buysellads etc.

3) **Search Traffic (Google & Bing):** These are type of traffic whereby the customers are actively searching for keywords and related terms to your offers. As a Newbie, you might want to start with Bing ads, master it and then try out Google ads. Google ads do require substantial budget due to high bidding, and they are usually very strict. Your ads account can easily be banned once you violate their Policies and Terms, and that could be a nightmare to you to create another ads account.

4) **Social Media Traffic (Facebook, Instagram & Pinterest):** This is also a high volume traffic source that you can master and really crush it with CPA Affiliate Marketing. The main place here is *Facebook*. The great thing about Facebook is its demographic targeting where you can target a particular demographic audience.

5) **Mobile Pop/Mobile Redirect Traffic (Pop ads, leadBolt etc):** This is basically Mobile traffic that pops up on mobile, usually when you are using apps on your mobile phone or visiting some websites. This is a sort of blind traffic with high volume, but costs less comparably, but usually may have low conversion rates.

6) **Press Releases:** Press releases ranks very well in Google Search and can bring you lots of Traffic if properly done. If you are a Beginner or Newbie, and do not Know how to Write Press Releases, you can always outsource them. I usually tell my Students, you don't necessarily need to be techy in everything, and so do not allow you're not being technical about a method deny you the benefits you could gain by doing it the right way. There are Freelancer Websites such as **FIVERR** that you can pay someone a little money as low as $5 to help you out with some Technical stuffs that can add to your ROI. I would usually recommend that you outsource Press Release articles for your affiliate offers on Fiverr, because it is one thing to write them and another to rank them. So, if you find someone who could do that, just ask them to insert

your affiliate links around the write Up, Maximum of Three Places. Your Press Release must sound Natural and not pushy, so that your readers can easily click through.

To outsource for your services on Fiverr, use the link below https://raygoz.com/fiverr

Take Note of this Tip: *"Focus on targeting mobile on all traffic Networks".* Mobile Traffic is **Cheap, Scalable** and does **Convert** Well.

TIPS FOR CREATING PROFITABLE CAMPAIGNS

In this part, am going to be sharing with you some tips you can implore to create and launch profitable campaigns especially as a Beginner or Newbie.

1) **Start off With International Traffic**: Usually, most offers are targeted towards USA, and as a Newbie, you most likely would be tempted to run offers in such highly competitive locations. As a Newbie, don't focus on USA traffic, if you do, you're likely going to be crushed, because the competition is way too

high. You may end up burning your money because of high bids, without necessarily getting results. Rather, start with offers that accepts International Traffic and bid for 2nd Tier traffic, which is relatively cheaper. It may interest you to know that some USA offers may have same payout for 2nd tier countries or even more, if you search deeper through the networks. You can target countries like Australia, Brazil, New Zealand, Norway etc.

2) **Mobile & Tablet Traffic is cheaper than Desktop traffic:** Focus more on mastering mobile traffic which is cheaper with most traffic networks. Mobile is relatively easy to browse on as well as easy going these days, so target Androids, iOS, Tablet etc. you can focus on one Mobile at a time when you are testing out offers.

3) **Start with Low payout offers:** as a Newbie, you don't want to start promoting high paying offers like $100 upwards, which require sales. You need huge budget to be profitable in promoting such kind of offers. Rather, you can start with lead generation

offers such as email submits, Surveys, Phone calls or Free Trial offers. Usually, you should go for $10 or less payout offers as a Newbie.

4) **Winning Campaigns are never found, they are Created:** you should always bear this fact in mind. Don't ever think you will find winning campaigns, but rather you will create them by tweaking some variables. You would have to optimize your campaigns and track them, thereby knowing exactly what is making you the money. Also bear this in mind that, 90% of campaigns you will launch may lose money at first, but over time, when you must have gathered enough data, you can be able to optimize your campaigns to make you Profits.

5) **Focus on Making one Spot Profitable First before Diversifying:** You don't want to be those people that tries to launch 20 different campaigns on 20 different spots on 20 different traffic sources, with 100 different banners, 100 different landing pages and all that...LOL. You are definitely going to burn your money. Focus on a specific spot, specific traffic source before trying to diversify. Don't test

too much, else you will lose too much money. Make sure you are able to make one spot work and master it before moving unto the next traffic spot.

6) **Test Tightly (Maximum of 5 Ads, 2LPs, 2 offers):** a lot of people starts running loads of offers and gets trigger happy, but in the actual sense of it, they might be losing money. When you Test tightly as recommended, you would be able to know what **Facts** is and what's **Fluke** through the data you would have gathered, which will enable you to make decisions.

7) **Track Absolutely Everything:** The Truth is; **"if you don't Track, you don't know"**. If you do not track your campaigns to know exactly what's making you money or not, you would possibly lose money. Two trackers I can recommend to you to use for your tracking is TestEasily or CPVLab. With this, you can focus on the variable that makes you most of the money.

8) **Look at Profit not ROI and Evaluate Everything on an EPC vs. CPC Basis:** EPC is your earnings per click,

while CPC is your cost per click. If your CPC is greater than your EPC, then you are basically losing money, but if they are both equal, then you are kind of at point of *Break even*, so you might consider to stop running the campaign at that point.

Watch This Tutorial Video below to learn more About CPA Marketing.

https://youtu.be/WZPnr1v4CDE

CHECKLIST FOR SUCCEDING WITH CPA MARKETING

- ✓ A high Converting Offer
- ✓ A targeted Interested audience
- ✓ A high converting Landing Page
- ✓ A tracking Software (Track everything)
- ✓ An Auto Responder (to build an email List)
- ✓ A Hunger to Succeed (Taking massive Action)

SOME TOOLS YOU REQUIRE FOR CPA MARKETING

In this part, I will be sharing with you some of the tools you may likely need in CPA Affiliate marketing. However, It is not compulsory to have all of them, but atleast some are very necessary for you, so I will highlight some of the tools here.

Domain Name and Hosting Plan

A Domain Name is simply the url to your website such as (www.example.com). There are many Registrars where one can Purchase Domain Names such as Godaddy, NameACheap etc, but for this Report, I would recommend BlueHost where you can get a Free Domain Name as well as a Hosting Plan.

BlueHost is being recommended because it is Tested and Trusted, and Reliable too, and it is a very Wordpress-friendly Hosting Plan. To Get Started, you can use my customized link below which gives you Discounts and Bonuses too.

https://www.raygoz.com/hosting

The above link is an affiliate link, and it does not cost you anything to use it, rather it gives you Discounts, Bonuses and Access to our Premium

Trainings, so I appreciate it if you Use the Link anytime you are ready to sign up.

Inside of the Bluehost plans, I also recommend going for the **Plus Plan**, which gives you access to Unlimited Websites and Unmetered Space for your websites. It gives you much more value for your Money.

Use the link below to access our full Training on how to set up your Websites in Few Minutes.

https://youtu.be/u4caFNVceaA

In choosing your Domain Name, take into consideration the Niche Market in which you are about to venture into or type of products you want to promote. Your Niche could be Health and Fitness, Make Money Online, Games, Movies, Dieting, etc. Usually, you should choose a Domain name that is generic to the Niche you wish to start promoting Products from, Example, in the Skincare Niche, you could use www.perfectskinlook.com or something related, that can be used to promote several products from that Niche. It does not have to be too specific for a Particular Product, I hope you got the Idea...Does that Make Sense..? Fantastic!

Software for Cloaking Your Affiliate Links

Most times, Google, Facebook, YouTube and several other Networks do not allow you to paste your Raw Affiliate Links on their Platform. Most of the times, you will get Banned. In order to overcome this hassle, you can use a software to cloak your Affiliate Links. In this Report, am going to be revealing to you a **SECRET Software** to do that, which is **FREE**, and Most Affiliates Do not Know About that. Most Cloaking Software out there are very expensive.

So, we shall be using a WordPress Plugin called *Pretty links*. This can only be installed when you already have your Wordpress Account set up through the first step above by Setting up your Hosting Plan Using BlueHost.

Here is a Video Tutorial to walk you through on how to Install the Plugin and start cloaking your Affiliate Links right away, and make them look like they are pages on your website.

https://youtu.be/rTOO6jH1e3c

Auto Responder (To Build an Email List)

You may have heard the saying that **"Money is in the List"** This is so True, and I can't over emphasize on how this is a very powerful skill to learn as long as Affiliate Marketing is concerned, and other forms of marketing too. When you build a list, you have an asset which you can market to at a click of a button. Many a times when customers visits a landing page or offer page, they may not convert immediately or make any purchase. But when you capture their emails using a lead capture page, you can build relationship with your list, remarket the products to them and even have the opportunity to promote related products to that list in future.

To Sign Up for an Auto Responder, you can use the link below:

www.bit.ly/get_autoresponder

CONCLUSION

If you don't take **ACTION** after reading this Report, nothing happens/changes. Visit the **links** I dropped in this Book, you can copy them and paste on your browser if you are not able to visit them directly here, especially the training Links, that is how you will get the Best out of this Guide, I didn't want to bore you with so much write up, watching video Tutorials is a more effective and practical way to Learn.

I hope you got Great Value from this brief report, as I stated earlier; short, simple, straight to the point and Actionable.

Cheers to Your Success,
Raymond.

CONNECT WTH ME
Website: https://raygoz.com
Facebook: https://facebook.com/raygozdigital
Email: nwachukwuchigozie11@gmail.com
Phone: +2348169575994.